Viktors Vrublevskis

How to teach reading to the Net Generation Children

How to teach reading for those
who do not want to read

Anchor Compact

Vrublevskis, Viktors: How to reach reading to the Net Generation Children: How to teach reading for those who do not want to read. Hamburg, Anchor Academic Publishing 2014
Original title of the thesis: «buchtitel»

Buch-ISBN: 978-3-95489-226-6
PDF-eBook-ISBN: 978-3-95489-726-1
Druck/Herstellung: Anchor Academic Publishing, Hamburg, 2014

Bibliografische Information der Deutschen Nationalbibliothek:
Die Deutsche Nationalbibliothek verzeichnet diese Publikation in der Deutschen Nationalbibliografie; detaillierte bibliografische Daten sind im Internet über http://dnb.d-nb.de abrufbar

Bibliographical Information of the German National Library:
The German National Library lists this publication in the German National Bibliography. Detailed bibliographic data can be found at: http://dnb.d-nb.de

All rights reserved. This publication may not be reproduced, stored in a retrieval system or transmitted, in any form or by any means, electronic, mechanical, photocopying, recording or otherwise, without the prior permission of the publishers.

Das Werk einschließlich aller seiner Teile ist urheberrechtlich geschützt. Jede Verwertung außerhalb der Grenzen des Urheberrechtsgesetzes ist ohne Zustimmung des Verlages unzulässig und strafbar. Dies gilt insbesondere für Vervielfältigungen, Übersetzungen, Mikroverfilmungen und die Einspeicherung und Bearbeitung in elektronischen Systemen.

Die Wiedergabe von Gebrauchsnamen, Handelsnamen, Warenbezeichnungen usw. in diesem Werk berechtigt auch ohne besondere Kennzeichnung nicht zu der Annahme, dass solche Namen im Sinne der Warenzeichen- und Markenschutz-Gesetzgebung als frei zu betrachten wären und daher von jedermann benutzt werden dürften.

Die Informationen in diesem Werk wurden mit Sorgfalt erarbeitet. Dennoch können Fehler nicht vollständig ausgeschlossen werden und die Diplomica Verlag GmbH, die Autoren oder Übersetzer übernehmen keine juristische Verantwortung oder irgendeine Haftung für evtl. verbliebene fehlerhafte Angaben und deren Folgen.

Alle Rechte vorbehalten

© Anchor Academic Publishing, ein Imprint der Diplomica® Verlag GmbH
http://www.diplom.de, Hamburg 2014

ABSTRACT

The topic of the research paper is "Effective Teaching Reading Techniques in Form Six." The paper consists of 45 pages, 4 chapters, 5 subchapters, 6 tables, 6 figures and 6 appendices. The author of the paper has analysed different kinds of sources, such as scientific research and publications, scientific and course books referred to the teaching reading methods and approaches. In his practical research the author has tried to practise the most effective methods and approaches. All authors's encountered successes and failures have been described, analysed and taken into consideration.

The author of the paper has chosen the reading topic because he discovered the contradiction between a great number of English lessons, qualitative course books, and usually poor reading skills in form six of non English-speaking class. The main positive conclusion is that variations of teaching methods' greatly improve reading skills, but at the same time this regularity does not always apply to the children having particular psychological problems like shyness, diffidence, fear. And finally, poor conclusion making ability and poor vocabulary is the main cause of poor reading and language comprehension.

TABLE OF CONTENT

INTRODUCTION 1
CHAPTER 1 3
   SUBCHAPTER 1.1 5
CHAPTER 2 8
   SUBCHAPTER 2.1 10
   SUBCHAPTER 2.2 14
   SUBCHAPTER 2.3 16
   SUBCHAPTER 2.4 17
CHAPTER 3 20
CHAPTER 4 31
LIST OF LITERATURE 33

INTRODUCTION

Reading is one of the most significant language skills which should be taught at elementary school. One significant difference between reading and other language skills is that readable text is on some surface and readers have time to reread and comprehend words, sentences they do not understand immediately. People often read in various ways for various purposes. For example unskilled nonnative readers do not read an English text entirely; instead of this they often carefully translate the text word by word, forgetting or not realizing that the main aim of reading is comprehension of a text.

Consciously or unconsciously, people frequently read to get some specific information or to understand the general idea of what a text or an article is about. When people read whole texts, they may also read in different ways, at different speed, depending usually on whether they are reading an easy tale for pleasure or a complicated text for work or study. In contemporary schools pupils are being taught various reading techniques, but even at secondary school they usually have to work hard to comprehend a text.

The basic school program usually involves learning the following reading techniques: scanning, skimming, reading for matching and reading for sequencing, but even these methods do not provide sufficient understanding of a text. Many coursebooks nowadays contain really entertaining texts, like the ones about computer games, travelling, and modern techniques; sometimes they include authentic materials from magazines, newspapers and books. Such course books are invented by the leading educational specialists in order to make reading more realistic, entertaining and effective. A number of texts include cognates which certainly motivate young learners to read and make a text more recognizable. It is sometimes difficult to get learners to read some short stories when they are on summer holidays, it usually leads to the degradation in reading skill.

The paper is divided into several logically related chapters in order to discover all possible factors which influence the process of mastering reading. The first part deals with the basic-school age pupils` psychological features. The second part discovers reading methods and the approaches which provide an effective teaching reading. The third part is about the author's own experience of being a teacher and attempts to practise the methods above-mentioned in the sixth form. And the last part consists of the main conclusions drawn from the paper. The author of the paper has used scientific reports, research articles and the books of the leading native and foreign psychologists, educational specialists referred to the process of reading.

The subject of the study is effective reading methods.

The objective of the research is to study effective teaching reading methods and their application s in form six.

The tasks of the research are as follows:
1. Study psychological and methodological literature related to the research topic.
2. Discover causes and effects of motivation.
3. Analyse different reading methods and their effectiveness.
4. Use reading methods practically.

The research methods are as follows:
1. A study and an analysis of the related literature and school documentation.
2. Manipulation of data

Hypothesis:
1. Implementation of various, effective reading methods improves students' reading abilities.

CHAPTER 1

At the age of 11 or 12 many pupils reach the so-called the stage of concrete operations (6-12 years). The psychologist James W. Kalat (16; 375) says that about at the age of seven children enter the stage of concrete operations and begin to understand the conversation about physical properties.

During these years cognitive development is very intensive. But James W. Kalat (16; 375) adds that at the stage of concrete operations, children can perform mental operations on concrete objects but still have trouble with abstract or hypothetical ideas. Children are usually very flexible at this age. The psychologist Lisa Oakley (18; 29) accentuates that the failure to complete complex tasks was due to the memory, failure-children were not able to remember what solutions they had tried. (see figure 1.1.)

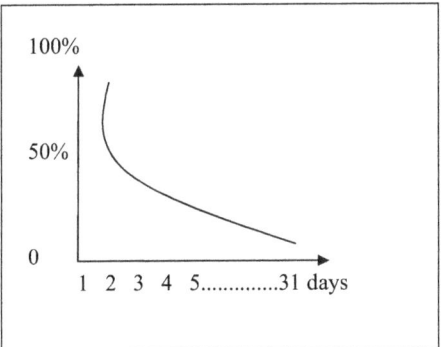

Figure 1.1 **Information storage** (36; 63)

James W. Kalat (22; 375) adds that the children do not reach the stage of formal operations more suddenly than they reach the concrete operations stage. Nevertheless some children show evidences of the formal operation stage in the form six. But professor Eysenck (22; 531) accentuates that initially Piaget argued that formal operation stage starts at the age of 11 or 12, but later he and other researches found out that most children of this age showed very little evidence of formal operations. The American psychologist Dennis M. McInerney (6; 137) concludes that recent studies indicate, however, that some of these ages need to be revised downwards. According to Piaget (16; 375) children reach the formal operations stage at about the age of 11. "But later researchers found that many people take longer to reach this stage and some never reach it". This is what the psychologist James W. Kalat said about such an ambiguous border between the concrete and formal stages. (16; 375)

Children usually spend much time thinking about and sorting through their experiences from school and sometimes they may seem serious. Linda Goldman (9; 7) says that during the formal operation stage a child is very curious about the concepts of death, and he or she seeks new realistic information. Cognitive development occurs in individual's cognitive structures, abilities and processes. Pupils are different at this age, but at the same time they have similarities. (see figure 1.2) Professor Pipere (24; 70) argues that age, aptitude, cognitive style, motivation, and personality are general factors, which are characteristic of all learners. Nevertheless some general factors are likely to change during the course of foreign language acquisition. Demands are high at basic school. Basic-school-age children's cognitive features must be taken into consideration. Professor Thomas P. Rohlen (32; 174) says that it is impossible to redouble children's attention if the lesson is repetitious and uninteresting, adding that teachers should present interesting problems; they pose numerous questions they probe and guide. According to this James W. Kalat (16; 375) says that children develop mental processes that deal with abstract, hypothetical situations and those processes demand logical, deductive reasoning and systematic planning.

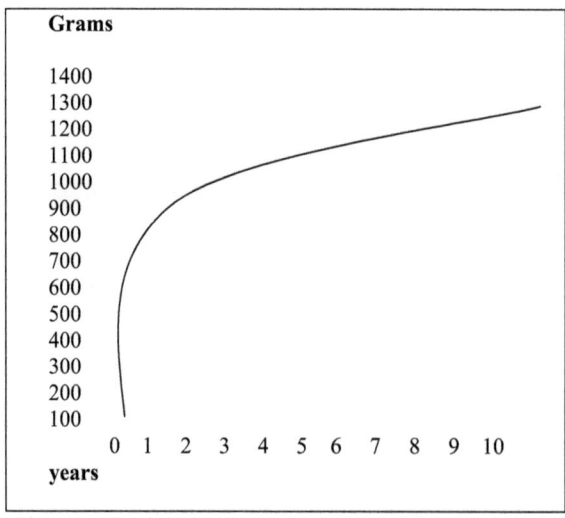

Figure 1.2 **Brain's development** (35; 99)

It is acknowledged that the Swiss biologist and psychologist Jean Piaget was the pioneer of cognitive development theory. The succeeding generations of educators built their theories upon the facts discovered by him. The great majority of western psychologists and educational specialists acknowledge Piaget's authority. This important theory was created by him in the last century! And only recently some researches have doubted his theory but nevertheless Piaget's influence on education is deep and pervasive. He championed a way of thinking about children that provided the foundation for today's education psychology. The Piaget opponents' the only one demerit against his theory is the age when children reach a particular stage. But that's no wonder because children have been accelerating rapidly for the past twenty years. The main difference between the concrete operator and the formal operator is the latter's ability to think abstractly.

SUBCHAPTER 1.1

Motivation is very significant. Timothy V. Rasinski (33 ;1) saying about the importance of motivation to read adds that motivation to read must be an essential goal in reading instruction programs for the 21-st century. There are various definitions of motivation but generally, they do not differ in meaning. The researcher Yasmin.B.Kafai (8; 443) defines motivation as the state of mind that initiates, directs, and sustains a certain activity. Usually the better motivated students have more chances to become skilled readers. Yasmin.B.Kafai (8; 443) adds that recent studies on literacy development show that reading motivation is a crucial factor for successful reading comprehension. But Skrinda (24; 72) holds the converse opinion stressing that it does not mean that better motivated learners will necessarily be more successful, but that on average they are more likely to be so.

Very often motivation to read means whether the text topic is interesting for children or not. It is natural that a more interesting text is going to be more motivating to read. As factors which reduce motivation to read Michael Pressley (21; 372) mentions difficult words in text, too complicated stories. James Hoffman (11; 61) says that most young children approach books eagerly because the pictures are appealing and joint books reading is usually an enjoyable social interaction. The philologist Skrinda (24; 70) accentuates that motivation and needs have always had a central place in theories of foreign language acquisition. Motivating students to read the text is something teachers need to begin to do before reading.

There are a lot of factors which form and develop motivation to read. It is not compulsory to use only course books. The researcher Paul Davies (23; 95) says that learners themselves can buy a different book each and build up a class library. It gives pupils the opportunity to choose reading material by themselves. That is why the reading expert Rona F. Filipo (28; 137) says that motivation for reading is promoted when teachers supported students' choice of learning tasks and involvement in decision making about learning activities.

Prior to a reading activity a teacher should choose an "observation point". To get students interested Dr. Robert D. Postman (26; 332) recommends teachers to stand where he or she can, see the entire class, ask questions to the whole class and then call on individuals for a response and gain attention trough the eye contact or a gesture. During the course of reading a teacher is looking to the process. It's very significant for teachers not to forget to laud pupils in case of their progress. An educational specialist Michael Pressley (21; 372) says that being recognized as a good reader can affect motivation to read, being a better reader than others can motivate reading and working at becoming an even better reader. During the lesson a teacher should use various approaches, tasks to keep pupils' interest. Naturally it is a hard work and a teacher must be well-prepared for it. Professor Rohlen (32; 174) says that teachers in Japan, knowing that children benefit from different teaching techniques, change their approach several times during every class period.

Some teachers can not permanently motivate pupils. It is obvious that parents' involvement in home reading improves reading skills. "But reading is something they can do at home, and you should encourage this as much as possible". This is what the researcher Paul Davies recommends teachers in order to involve pupils' parents in reading. (23; 95) "The analysis of different forms of cooperation showed that at schools where more parents' meetings and discussions about a child's improvement were held together with the child, students' academic success was on average higher than in other schools". This is how the educator of Tallinn Pedagogical University Lukk describes interaction between parents and their children. (5; 96) The associate professor of teacher development Timothy V. Rasinski (33; 1) recognizes the importance of home-school connections, especially for the development of engaged and enthusiastic readers. The additional reading at home stimulates motivation, but the home-reading should not be a punishment for a child. Timothy V. Rasinski (33; 1) concludes that when the home is involved, both reading achievement and children's love for reading increase. Motivation is a very complex process depending on many factors which should be taken into account. James V. Hoffman (11; 62) believes that the motivation to read is the result of a complex interaction among child's history and abilities, the features of the text, the purpose for reading, the social conditions and support surrounding the activity. Every teacher should remember what affects reading motivation. Yasmin. B. Kafai (8; 443) says that many factors influence student's reading motivation including self-efficacy, outcome expectations, goals, value beliefs regarding to reading and interests in topics. Every teacher must realize the need for motivating students. The educational researcher Yasmin.B.Kafai (8; 443) says that in actual classroom settings, however, teachers' perception has also been used as a major source for accessing students' motivation for reading.

If a teacher was able to motivate students, they would certainly achieve high results in reading comprehension. An educational specialist Jane Braunger (12; 72) says that a motivated individual initiates and continues a particular activity, returning to a task with sustained engagement, even when it becomes difficult. Parents usually have much influence with their children and this factor must be used by teachers. The associate professor of teacher development Timothy V. Rasinski (33; 1) reminds that reading achievement is highly correlated with the amount of time spent out of school on reading. The author of the paper thinks that motivation is one of the leading factors providing successful reading in English but not the only one. The motivated readers achieve high results in reading. Teachers cannot permanently motivate pupils. At the same time teachers must cooperate with learners' parents and encourage them to motivate their children.

To encourage an interest in reading, one of the best things a teacher can do is share his or her own love of reading with students. A teacher should talk about books that he or she read in childhood. A teacher can also find out what books his or her students read for pleasure. It is important to send the message to students that a teacher values and enjoys reading. A teacher should encourage students to find answers to their own questions by reading texts. Sometimes it is important to use books which include stories, bright pictures, because at this age children like bright pictures and heroes on the pages.

CHAPTER 2

Reading came to life later than speaking or writing. The psychologist Keith Rayner (17; 36) says that in contrast, writing is a relatively recent human activity and the ability to read and write was not produced by biological change but by cultural change. The educational consultant Dr. David Sousa (3; 205) says that it is not easy to master reading because there is no reason to consider reading to be a natural ability like speaking.

The researcher Paul Davies (23; 100) says that reading has much in common with listening but the text is permanent which may make it easier to understand. Various specialists give different descriptions of reading. For example, Widdowson (1; 192) says that reading is not a reaction to a text but an interaction between a writer and a reader mediated trough a text. Another professor of Education Christopher Brumfit (1; 192) considers reading as an ability to interact with a text by decoding the language and comprehending the concepts presented. And finally the psychologist Keith Rayner (17; 23) says that reading is the ability to extract visual information from the page and comprehend the meaning of the text. The essential idea presented by all these specialists is that reading is the interaction between a writer and a reader. Nevertheless, readers do not master the effective reading techniques at once.

As stated above, reading has much in common with listening but nevertheless reading is used together with other skills. A linguistic specialist Coreen Sears (2; 165) says that a variety of authentic literature is used in the teaching of reading, associated with extension activities that require students' responses in speech and writing, and the performance of meaningful tasks. While reading a text, it does not necessarily mean that the reader is focusing attention on a particular word or letter. Researches describe this process very exceptionally. The psychologist Keith Rayner (17; 181) states that the amount of information that could be possessed on a fixation is shown to be fixated word plus some additional information to the right of it. Keith Rayner (17; 181) adds that fluent reading is based on generating guesses or hypothesis about what the next word is. (see figure 2.1)

It is necessary to concentrate one's attention only on reading process. The psychologist Keith Rayner (17; 195) says that if the reader's speech tract is somehow concurrently engaged during reading, he or she will not be able to subvocalize the text material.

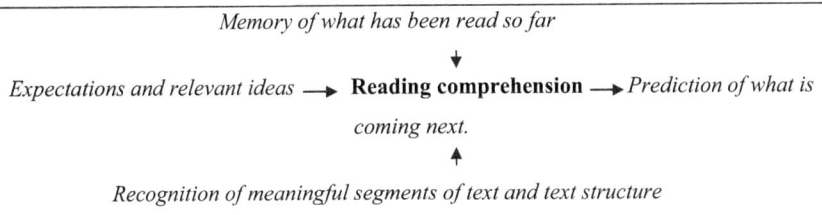

Figure 2.1 **The functioning of the fluent reading** (23; 91)

Pupils can read aloud or silently, depending on the purpose of reading. Both the types have their advantages and disadvantages. "One advantage of having subjects read aloud is that one potentially has a record of what has been processed. This is one can see whether the reader is making mistakes and can also determine what mistakes are being made". This is how the psychologist Keith Rayner sums up the advantages of reading aloud. (17; 180) The home education consultant Jessie Wise (13; 359) says that having a child read aloud increases his vocabulary, expands his general knowledge and forces him to figure out new words, and it also allows teachers to correct errors before they become habits. The psychologist Keith Rayner (17; 180) adds that another obvious method for studying reading "on-line" is to have people read aloud and record their vocal output, so that both its accuracy and the time course of the vocal output can be analysed. The inner speech should be activated because it provides comprehension of a text while reading silently. The psychologist Keith Rayner (17; 216) says that inner speech serves a useful function in reading comprehension. Keith Rayner (17; 181) also adds that reading aloud is only about half the speed of silent reading. "When we read silently, we often experience the feeling of hearing our voice saying the words our eyes are falling down. Some readers actually move their lips at times during silent reading and there is a considerable amount of muscle activity in the speech tract". This is how the psychologist Keith Rayner describes silent reading. (17; 188). Nevertheless, Kleiman (17; 196) argues that the meaning of individual words can be obtained without reference to inner speech. No matter what reading methods are used, a frequent reading practice must take place, otherwise much will be forgotten. The educational consultant Dr. David Sousa (3; 60) mentions that reading practice increases familiarity with the patterns of letters that form printed word, thereby improving spelling, improves comprehension, grammatical functions and pronunciation.

As far as possible, teachers should also use literary texts. The professor of Education Christopher Brumfit (1; 191) says that the English language teachers' main goal is to teach the grammar of the language, literature due to its structural complexity and its unique use of language. Another supporter of using literary texts Povey (1; 191) argues that literature increases all language skills, because literature extends linguistic knowledge by giving evidence of extensive and subtle vocabulary usage. Nevertheless, Christopher Brumfit (1; 192) says that the critics of the use of literature maintain to a great extent that literary texts reflect a particular cultural perspective; they may be difficult for students to read.

A reader interacts with a text to create its meaning. This is the effective reading. For example, A mother asked her son whether the book was entertaining or not. The son answered that he did not know. The mother asked him why he was lying to her. She said she heard that the son was reading aloud! The son answered that he was really reading it but he did not listen to himself. A reader must not be somehow concurrently engaged during reading. Even the chewing of a chewing-gum decreases reading comprehension.

On the whole, effective reading materials should contain literary texts. But they must be used in accordance with pupils' knowledge and needs. It is necessary to take a text seriously as all the instruction how to read and what to read. All the efforts will be in vain if a text does not entertain pupils. Pupils should read various texts in order to recognize the different text types and to prepare for an uncomplicated sentence structure, high-frequency vocabulary. Teachers should be patient, because full reading comprehension requires more knowledge of the language and higher level of reading skills.

SUBCHAPTER 2.1

The scientifically- based methods often guarantee successful instructions. The educational consultant Dr. David Sousa (3; 141) says that the students receiving instruction in scientifically-based programs demonstrate rapid growth in reading achievement. Two main methods are used in order to teach pupils basics of reading. The psychologist Keith Rayner (17; 348) says that these two primary methods used to teach children to read are whole word (or look-say) instruction and phonics instruction. The proponents of the look- say method consider it to be the leading one. Professor Michael Pressley (21; 154) adds that the look-say approach emphasizes students learning words as wholes rather than learning to decode via phonics. The educational professor Susan B. Neuman (31; 59) says that memorizing whole words may lead to rapid progress in early reading, particularly for children with good visual memories because some words encountered in early reading (such as *could, the*) have an irregular pattern of letter-sound mapping that requires whole word memorization. The Chief Scientist of Soliloquy doctor Marilyn Jager Adams (20; 38) says that children who were trained through the look-say method demonstrated an early advantage in rate and comprehension of silent reading and perhaps in interest, fluency, and expression as well. On the other hand, Susan B. Neuman (31; 59) concludes that whole-word memorization can initially jump start reading development, but relying on this approach may be problematic for long-term reading development. This method is usually appropriate for children with good visual memories. "Pictures are often used to associate letters with sounds. The child will see the letter *a*, then a picture of an apple. Learning a key picture is an extra mental step; children will easily go from seeing the symbol to saying the sound for which it stands". This is what the home education consultant Jessie Wise sums up about key pictures. (13; 358) The look and say method must be used; however, this is not the only way. The researcher Judith Orasanu (15; 1) says that the look-say method's role today is to aid in recognizing irregularly spelled words, while the alphabetic and phonetic aspects of the language remain dominant. Some researchers recognize the dominance of the phonics instruction.

The educational consultant Dr. David Sousa (3; 74) says that phonics instruction teaches the relationships between phonemes of the spoken language and the graphemes of the written language and how to use these relationships to read and write words. Marilyn Jager Adams (20; 38) says that children who were taught phonics, exhibited the early advantage of word recognition, particularly in untaught words, and maintained it throughout. Nonetheless David Sousa (3; 74) says that phonics instruction teaches children a system for remembering how to read words. Western researchers like Marilyn Jager Adams (20; 38) say that the programs that included systematic phonics resulted in significantly better word recognition, better spelling, better vocabulary, and better reading comprehension at least trough the first grade. The home education consultant Jessie Wise (13; 358) reminds that basic phonics sounds must be learnt. All that means, that the phonics instructions must be taught. David Sousa (3; 74) says that phonics instruction that is systematic and explicit makes a bigger contribution to a child's growth in reading than little or no phonics instruction, and it contributes to comprehension skills rather than inhibiting them. As well as the look and say method, the phonic instruction has its disadvantages. David Sousa (3; 74) says that some critics of phonics say that English spellings are too irregular for phonics instruction to be of any value, adding that phonics instruction beyond grade 6 is not generally productive for most students. Both the methods should be used. The educational consultant Dr. David Sousa (3; 142) reminds that many struggling readers can learn to read, they just need different kinds of instructional strategies. (see table 2.1.1)

Table 2.1.1 **Reading-aloud strategies** (23; 92-93)

	Strategy	*Effectiveness*
Echo reading	The tutor reads aloud one or two sentences and the learner repeats what the tutor has read, mimicking the tutor's speech patterns.	Imitating intonation and pacing helps the learner acquire the skills used by fluent readers.
Repeated reading	The learner reads and rereads familiar passages or parts of favourite books. By returning to the same material over time, the learner begins to recognize textual features, such as heading and subheadings.	This approach also helps the reader become increasingly aware of the relationships between symbols and sounds, thus increasing fluency. This strategic approach encourages confidence and fluency.
Partner reading	The tutor and the student take turns reading so that the student can hear parts of the text read fluently and have a short break from reading.	Taking turns reading out aloud helps students anticipate the words and ideas they will encounter when it becomes their turn to read.
Reading unison	The tutor and the student sit side by side and read the selection aloud in unison.	Reading in unison allows the student to read chunks of text at one sitting and to readily get meaning from what is read.
Reading to each other	Either the student or the tutor reads part of the text first. The listener then retells the selection that has just been read or the reader asks the questions about the selection. The reader and the student then reverse roles.	Dependent readers often enjoy finding questions that will stump their tutors

The statistics shows the effectiveness of both instructions. The educational specialist Herbert Ira London (10; 45) names the fact that in North Carolina 44 percent of students were becoming dyslexic because of the reading instruction that relied on a look-say method, while only 8 percent of students were becoming dyslexic at a private school in Florida that employed phonics method.

When readers become more skilled and confident, they use skimming and scanning for different purposes. The educator Vincent Douglas (34; 51) says that skimming is reading quickly to get a general idea of what a reading selection is about and scanning is looking for certain words to find facts or answer questions. The educational consultant Lori Jamison Rog (19; 144) says that good readers read in different ways and at different rates, depending on the purpose for reading and the type of a text. The researcher Paul Davies (23; 100) says that learners should be discouraged from reading or translating slowly word by word, adding that skimming and scanning are two approaches to reading which can be useful for specific purposes (getting a general idea, or finding specific information). The eye movement technique is a necessary part of skimming-scanning instructions. "When I want to quickly get a general sense of what a section of text is about, I run my eyes quickly over the page without focusing on specific words. This is called skimming". This is how Lori Jamison Rog instructs pupils in skimming. (19; 144) A teacher should not combine some activities in order to achieve higher results. The home education consultant Jessie Wise (13; 356) suggests not teaching comprehension concurrently with teaching the sound or printed letters because it diverts the child's attention from figuring out words phonetically. Reading must be combined with other skills in order to read efficiently. The researcher Paul Davies (23; 100) says that full reading comprehension, which is needed for serious study or work, requires more knowledge of the language and higher level of reading skills.

In form six some pupils read word by word. The great difficulties are inability to remember irregular words and pronunciation. At school pupils basically read in order to gain information or in order to understand the main idea. At home a student may also read for enjoyment. Unfortunately, reading at home is not popular among them. The aim for reading also determines the appropriate method to reading comprehension. In forms six it is enough to master at last skimming and scanning because some children read word by word as yet. Pupils have to know basic grammar rules, read literary texts in order to perform skimming. The text presents letters, words, grammar constructions and a reader uses knowledge, skills to determine what that meaning is. The purpose for reading and the type of text determine the specific knowledge, skills and strategies that readers need to apply to achieve comprehension.

SUBCHAPTER 2.2

Warm-up activities prepare students for the following reading. The educational professor Deborah P. Berrill (4; 84) concludes that the majority of time is spent on pre-reading strategies. The researcher Paul Davies (23; 92) says that this stage is to prepare the learners for what they are going to read, just as we are usually prepared in our real life. Deborah P. Berrill (4; 68) says that one of the most important goals of pre-reading activities is activating prior knowledge, adding that it helps to set a purpose for reading, so that before readers begin to read a text, they will be primed to look for specific information. If the pupils are prepared for reading, they will be able to comprehend a text better. The educational consultant Lori Jamison Rog (19; 144) says that this activity has the added value of introducing concepts and vocabulary that are necessary the background for the students.(see table 2.2.1)

Table 2.2.1 **Anticipation guide** (19; 148)

Before reading		*After reading*
_Agree _Disagree	People around the world have always loved chocolate	_Agree _Disagree
_Agree _Disagree	Chocolate grows on trees	_Agree _Disagree
_Agree _Disagree	Milk chocolate was created by mixing milk and chocolate	_Agree _Disagree
_Agree _Disagree	Chocolate was discovered about 500 years ago	_Agree _Disagree

Some pre-reading exercises should be done in order to activate pupils' prior knowledge. The home education consultant Jessie Wise (13; 356) says that seeing pictures with alphabet letters and key words may be useful as a pre-reading exercise.

It is also necessary to pay attention to the title in order to understand a text better. Jo Phenix (14; 16) suggests teachers to ask pupils to pay attention to a title before reading. Deborah P. Berrill (4; 69) reminds that for each tutoring session, tutors will generally choose only one pre-reading goal, such as drawing comparisons.

A teacher must know exactly what he or she wants to achieve by pre-reading. Deborah P. Berrill (4; 69) mentions some effective pre-reading strategies, such as focus questions, content analysis, graphic organizers, and semantic maps, thought webs, pyramid outlines and anticipation guides.

Pre-reading activities may take different forms. The educational professor Deborah P. Berrill (4; 68) says that preliminary discussions encourage learners to express their thoughts or feelings about what they are going to read and such discussions stimulate engagement with the text. "By helping learners make predictions, tutors not only prepare them for reading, but also model what independent readers do to anticipate textual meaning." This what Deborah P. Berrill reasons about making predictions before reading. (4; 69)

Pre-reading activities depend on the purpose of reading. The educational professor Deborah P. Berrill (4; 69) says that tutors may also use pre-reading activities to help learners practise reading skills, such as sequencing information, finding cause-and-effect relationships, drawing comparisons, making inferences, and learning new vocabulary. Teachers should plan all the details of a lesson in order to be confident during it. Deborah P. Berrill (4; 69) says that tutors need to be reminded to be realistic in their planning of strategy use, allocating anywhere from 5 to 15 minutes, depending on the familiarity of the topic and difficulty of the text.

Pupils must clearly understand the task. Deborah P. Berrill (4; 74) says that graphic organizers focus learners' attention on what they are about to read and help them to express and clarify their thoughts about the topic of the story before reading it. (see table 2.2.2)

Table 2.2.2 **Semantic map** (4; 76)

Cultural Significance	- **Blue Jeans** -	Origin and History
Worker		*Levi-Strauss*
Rebellion	|	*prospectors*
Designer		*rivets*
	Manufacturing	
	Rivets	
	Denim	
	Indigo	

Pre-reading means a body of assignments, done before reading, which provides the better comprehension of a text. The key to confidence in reading is to prepare children to read effectively. This means "warming them up", engaging their interest in the subject of the reading text, but also pre-teaching the words they will need to understand and enjoy the text. It is important to spend enough time before the learners begin the assignment. To achieve these aims teachers should vary their methods and pre-reading may take the form of class discussions, films, tapes, pictures, maybe writing. Sometimes pre-reading may be as free as possible.

SUBCHAPTER 2.3

In while-reading activities, students check their comprehension as they read. The researcher Paul Davies (23; 99) says that this stage is to help learners understand the text. Using anticipation guide approach (see table 2.3.1) a teacher can prepare pupils for while-reading. A teacher must observe the pupils while they are reading. "Posing question during the reading phase helps tutors determine how well their students understand the text. By answering this questions students determine what they do not understand and what they need to clarify". In such a way the educational professor Deborah P. Berrill describes the effectiveness of while-reading questions. (4; 84) There can be various kinds of while-reading instructions. "Now that you have thought about which of these statements you think are true, go on and read the whole article to see if you were right. At the end, we will talk about whether you changed your minds about any of the ideas". This is what the educational consultant Lori Jamison Rog suggests to perform just before the reading. (19; 149)

In general while-reading activities are not as deep and complex as pre-or post-reading activities. The researcher Paul Davies (23; 99) says that learners may first do an easy scanning or skimming task, and then a task requiring more thorough comprehension. It is important to control while - reading activities. But if the pupils are asking questions many times, such an activity will turn into a dialogue. The educational professor Deborah P. Berrill (4; 84) adds that dependent readers need to know that fluent readers ask questions while they read to create their own meaning- they are interacting with the text.

Somebody said that a teacher is an actor. For example, the educational professor Deborah P. Berrill (4; 86) adds that tutors can model how to ask questions while reading, sometimes to note a confusion, sometimes to wonder where to find out more information and sometimes to debate an idea expressed by the author. The researcher Paul Davies (23; 93) suggests the following while-reading ideas.

- Scan for two to four items of information,
- Skim for the general idea,
- Answer questions,
- Complete sentences,
- Complete a table, map, or picture,
- Ask each other questions.

It is possible to combine reading and writing in order to improve both skills. The educational professor Deborah P. Berrill (4; 87) adds that sometimes questions may be oral or written by hand. At the same time Paul Davies (23; 93) concludes that teachers should help learners to understand the text rather than just test their comprehension the whole time.

The purpose for reading determines the appropriate while-reading activities. It is important to conduct while-reading strategies sequentially. After students have read a text fragment, a teacher may use the following strategies. It is essential to ask them several questions in order to check their comprehension during the reading. Students may write a short summary of the text fragment. Students may also be given a series of combined sentences, which summarize the plot of a chapter and so on. The key is to use the tasks appropriate for them. In form six pupils like working in groups and texts with bright pictures. Another idea is that a teacher selects some simple sentences from different parts of the text and writes them on the board. Learners put them in the correct order and predict the story in groups. A teacher must be aware that such pictures will intrigue and entertain pupils. If pupils are interested in a while-reading task, the comprehension of a text improves.

SUBCHAPTER 2.4

The final stage of effective reading is post-reading. The researcher Paul Davies (23; 93) says that this stage is to help the learners to connect what they have read with their own ideas and experience and perhaps to move fluently from reading to another classroom activity. The educational consultant Lori Jamison Rog (19; 144) says that after-reading strategies help students to learn to distinguish key information from supporting details. The professor Rosalie Fink (29; 26) says that after-reading exercises deepen students' text comprehension and make reading experience memorable and fun. As usual, the oral part of post-reading strategies consists of comprehension questions. "Once a child is reading independently, you may start asking "who", "what", "when", "where" questions about material he has just read". This is what the education consultant Jessie

Wise urges on the importance of post-reading questions. (13; 358) The post-reading questions are the most widely used strategy because of time-saving. The researcher Paul Davies (23; 99) says that good post-reading activities usually involve listening or speaking and sometimes writing. The researcher Paul Davies (23; 93) suggests the following post-reading ideas.

- Discuss what was interesting or new in the text,
- Discuss or debate the topic of the text if it's controversial,
- Do tasks on the language or structure of the text,
- Summarize the text, either orally or in writing.

The post-reading questions make it possible to estimate the conception of the text read. But at the same time these questions do not develop so significant writing skills. The psychologist Rik Ruiter (25; 125) says that the post-reading stage requires teachers to expand the passage with various activities, such as role-plays, dramas, oral-reports, writing exercises, adding that even grammar exercises can be designed. It is significant to vary the types of the post-reading activities in order to keep up motivation. The educational specialist Roger.D.Sell (27; 304) supposes that pos-reading activities include text comprehension questions, which can be either oral or written, and which can be answered individually, in groups, or by the whole class.   The reading purpose determines the type of questions. The educational specialist Roger.D.Sell (27; 304) says that post-reading questions, focusing on language, content, or both, can be either literal- i.e. questions about information contained in the text-or inferential- i.e. questions about the points which are not explicit. Roger.D.Sell (27; 304) mentions the following post-reading activities.

- Text comprehension questions,
- Inferential questioning and discussion,
- Reader response in small groups and as a whole class,
- Reader response individually in written tasks,
- Various types of processes written individually,
- Presentations and products in groups and in a whole class,
- Drama activities.

Students should perform post-reading exercises in order to see the point deeper. In the end the educational specialist Donald Bear (7; 208) points out that post- reading technique is equally as effective with content area materials as with narratives.

The author of the paper considers that the primary goal of the post - reading phase is to help students to retain what they have individually created in their minds from the text. Post reading actions also provide deeper memorization and understanding of a text. There are various strategies which provide the better comprehension of a text such as answering questions, summarizing main ideas, drawing conclusions or applying the information to a new situation. After reading a particular text, students need to have ways to organize and sort information in order to remember it. If they can not remember what they have read, then they have not learned from this reading.

CHAPTER 3

The author of the paper completed the pedagogical practice at Secondary school No.1 in form six. All the pupils participated in the research were non-native English speakers. The author's qualification practise took place from the 5th of March till the 3rd of April 2007. The author of the paper conducted three experimental reading lessons and ten common ones during his qualification practise. Every common lesson contained at least one reading exercise. The author used the course books, such as "Opportunities-elementary", "Discoveries 2", short tales, letters, and advertisements as reading materials.

This is the Russian language speaking class, which consists of 8 boys and 9 girls. The boys' hobbies generally were football, computer games and techniques. The girls were commonly interested in dancing, cooking and fashion. It is necessary to know their interests in order to prepare the appropriate texts for the reading lessons.

Four pupils, including one boy were skilled in English, ten pupils had an average knowledge and the last three ones were poor in English. Such a conclusion is drawn taking into consideration the pupils' personal performance and the marks received. The two non-achievers had good knowledge in English, but they had some psychological problems, such as shyness and fear to read aloud. These psychological problems did not allow them to learn efficiently. These pupils usually showed poor reading skills, but they were good at grammar. The possible reason for it was the fear to read aloud being in the centre of attention. Working individually with those pupils, the author assured himself in their good English knowledge.

In the practical part of the work the author has decided to use theoretical approaches and methods described in the theoretical part of the paper. Therefore, the author has used tasks for elementary level students (form 6), which would follow the theoretical principles such as: authenticity of the texts, different types of tasks and reading comprehension.

In the students' books for elementary level, students (form 6) are offered following while-reading activities:
 -read the text and match the paragraphs with the titles,
 -match the topics with the parts of the article,
 -in what order did they do these activities,
 -complete the sentences with the words from the text,
 -complete the table with the nouns and verbs from the text,
 -are these statements true or false,

-read the text and list the advantages of each gadget according to the adverts,
-find three 'facts' and three 'opinions' in the adverts,
-find examples for these linking words in the text,
-complete the table with adjectives from the advertisements,
-match this information with the words in blue in the text, these are called 'hot words', on a real Internet page you can 'click' on the words to get more information,
-put the sentences below in the correct gaps in the text,
-make compound words by matching one from each list, use the text,
-which of these things can you find in the text,
-put the events in the correct order,
-match the characters with the actions.

These activities are good and interesting for students. There are different kinds of texts and topics in the students' books, but each text has only one or two while-reading activities. The most difficult issue was to apply appropriate while-reading activities.

The students' text comprehension level in English was evaluated in this form. In order to do it, the author of the present work used different checking techniques such as testing of students, questionnaires, semantic maps, comprehension questions, roleplays, discussions. In order to have a basis for evaluation of everybody's reading skills, the author made an effort to work out levels that corresponded to definite degrees of text comprehension and degree of participation. The criteria for level definitions were as follows:

High level-can comprehend about 70-100% of a text; can extract key information on specific points by skimming the text and listening to the text.
Middle level-can comprehend about 45-69% of a text; can understand the gist by scanning the text.
Low level- can comprehend about 20-44% of a text; can identify the main idea only of a simple text.

In order to evaluate students reading skills the students were asked to read the text and to do the tasks. The three experimental lessons' texts were intended to check up the students' reading comprehension.

Table 3.1 **First experimental lesson's plan**

Sequence	Time (minutes)	Activity	Content
1	5	"Warm-up" activities	Homework analysis," warm-up" questions.
2	10	Pre-reading	"Agree-disagree" and comprehension pre-reading questions.
3	5	Reading a text	The history of computers.(about 200 words)
4	5	While-reading	Writing exercise
5	10	Post-reading	Filling in a crossword puzzle
6	5	Questionnaire	Exercises which helped students understand the content of the story

The tasks of the lesson were: to use vocabulary of nouns, related to the topic, to read and understand an article, to understand pronoun references in a text, to practice verb – noun collocations. The main objective of this lesson was to check students' text comprehension level and find out the appropriate approaches for it.

Before starting any exercise it was necessary to raise the pupils' interest in the subject of the lesson. Firstly, the author of the research paper started asking them some general warm-up questions, unrelated to the topic of the lesson, such as "What is the day today?", "Who is absent today?' "Did you have any difficulties in your homework?" Later on the author introduced the topic of the reading lesson, its schedule and exercises.

The pre-reading exercise was the vocabulary one. The students were asked to listen to the key words-parts of the body and verbs of sensation. Then they read the key words and checked the meaning of new words in the Mini-dictionary. After that the students worked in pairs and matched the verbs of sensation with the parts of body. The author checked the students' answers by asking individuals to say full sentences, e.g. I see with my eyes, we use our fingers to touch objects.

Having answered these questions the pupils were asked to read a text and write three ways computers can help disabled people. The students worked individually, the author explained that the article describes more than three ways computers help disabled people, so students had to choose three of these for their sentences. The author told students to try and guess the meaning of any new words that they think are important or look them up in the Mini-dictionary. The author checked students' answers by asking individuals to read aloud their sentences. There are some examples of possible answers: Computers can help blind people see using their ears; Computers can help blind people see by touching the screen and feeling images.

Having read the text, they started filling in the crossword puzzle containing the main parts of the computer, such as a monitor, a system unit, a keyboard. The crossword results, correct answers, text comprehension level and pupils` activity were assessed by giving every pupil one mark. At the end of the lesson the students had to fill in the questionnaires. The students were asked about the activities which helped them understand the content of the story. (see figure 3.1)

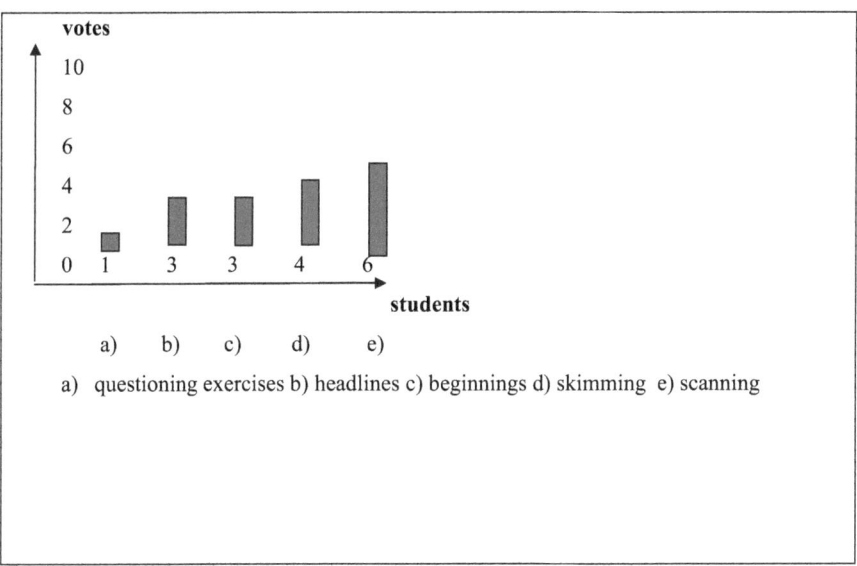

Figure 3.1 **Exercises that helped students understand the content of the story.**

The analysis of the lesson. As it seen in Figure 3.1, 3 students pointed out headline exercises useful, 4 students believed that skimming for main ideas helped them understand the content, 3 students asserted beginnings useful, while 6 considered scanning for details useful. Only the one student found questioning exercises very helpful.

Reading is an active skill. It constantly involves guessing, predicting, checking, asking and answering questions. This should be taken into consideration when devising reading comprehension exercises. Another important point is that the author has considered was that the activities were flexible and varied. The aim of the exercises was clearly defined. One of the most important things was that students were interested in what they read. It was very useful for students' motivation.

The better motivated students usually have more chances to become skilled readers. Pre-reading activities inspired the pupils. This text required particular pre-reading activities. Before reading the text the research paper author activated students' knowledge, provided vocabulary instruction, explained purposes for reading. Before doing the task, pupils must know the problem specification. If they do not realize how to do a task, they will certainly disturb the reading process itself. The author tried to explain the problem specifications in details. Having asked them the while-reading comprehension questions about the general idea of the text, the author concluded that their understanding was various. For example, the better comprehenders were able to access information quickly and accurately.

The post-reading exercise showed a fuller picture of their comprehension. In order to fill in the crossword puzzle, it was necessary to scan the text for searching the titles of the main parts of the computer. Without understanding the meaning of the words, there was almost no comprehension. The author has assured himself that the poor readers still had weakness in vocabulary, even if the pre-reading exercise had been done. Most of them did not complete the crossword puzzle or did it improperly. They also took longer to learn the grammar base, reading instructions and showed poorer retention of it over time. But it is necessary to note, that all the pupils showed better comprehension when they were assisted to find the relevant part of the text. Having analysed the post-reading exercise, the author drew the following conclusions. The poor readers were not able to make an inference, even when they were encouraged to search the text in order to find the specific information needed, from which to make a conclusion. The poor readers were also weak at answering the questions about the stories, main ideas, suggesting that their deficiency of the text comprehension was not only the consequence of their inability to draw conclusions. The second aspect of successful reading was knowledge.

Table 3.2 **The second experimental lesson's plan**

Sequence	Time (minutes)	Activity	Content
1	5	" Warm-up" activities	Homework analysis, warm-up questions
2	10	Pre-reading	A written exercise
3	10	Reading a text	A story about the animals, people have domesticated.(about 200 words)
5	10	Post-reading	Listening to the tape and writing down animals, living in our country
6	5	Questionnaire	Activities which helped them analyse and remember the vocabulary better

The tasks of the lesson were: to use vocabulary of nouns, related to the names of animals, to read and understand an article, to link the different language skills through the chosen reading activities, to practice verb – adjective collocations.

The objectives of the lesson were: to acquire grammar patterns and vocabulary items, to read and understand the text, to write and speak about animals.

First of all, the research paper author informed the students on the topic of the reading lesson. The author started the lesson with general warm-up questions, such as" Who is absent today? ","What is the weather like today? "," Have you prepared your homework?" The author inquired them about their homework, whether it was difficult or not. The pre-reading exercise was the written one. The pupils had to write all possible animals, sorting them from the biggest to the smallest ones. The aim of this exercise was to test their vocabulary on this topic and writing skills. Having written the names of animals, each student read them out. The next student read out the animals which were not named before. While reading the letter, the author was asked usual questions about unknown words.

The post-reading exercise took the form of the test, where the students had to listen to the tape with a story and write down the animals' titles. The test results, the writing exercises, the text comprehension level and pupils' activity were assessed by giving every student one mark. Then, the students were asked which of the activities the students ever completed, helped them analyse and remember the vocabulary better. (see figure 3.2)

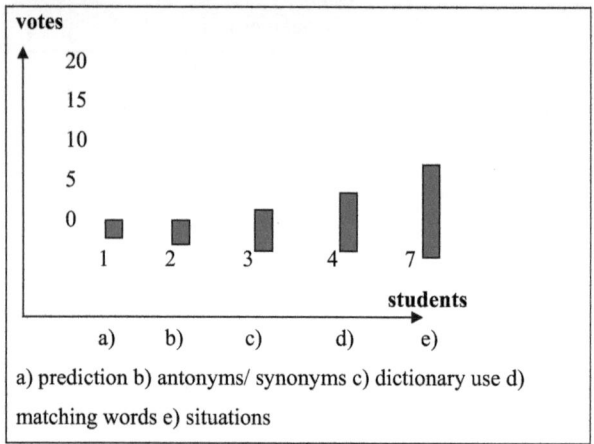

Figure 3.2 **Exercises that helped students analyze and remember the vocabulary better**

The analysis of the lesson. As figure 3.2 shows, 3 students marked dictionary use exercises as very helpful, in memorizing the vocabulary, 1 student pointed out prediction exercises. However, 4 of the students found the exercises where they had to match words with their definition very helpful, 2 students stated, that they memorized the vocabulary by finding antonyms and synonyms to the given words in the text . The majority of the students (7) considered they gained benefit from situations using the new vocabulary.

With these classroom tasks, the author helped students develop the reading skill as well as other skills like speaking, writing, listening and language areas like vocabulary and grammar. The students were prepared for the text. Reading comprehension was not separated from the other skills. The author linked the different skills through the chosen reading activities: reading and writing, listening and writing, reading and speaking. The text contained grammar patterns and vocabulary items and reinforced basic knowledge.

The written exercise indicated the pupils' poor vocabulary and spelling errors. The positive moment was that such a group exercise increased their interest in reading the following text. Group tasks always motivated the students and engaged their interest in the subject.

This lesson's text was read without a dictionary. Reading without a dictionary has its features. Tthe author has concluded that the more pupils read without a dictionary, the more comprehension increased in the vocabulary knowledge. It was truth when a text contained the words which had been earlier learned but were partly forgotten. The reason for it was that the readers did not know the meaning of all the words presented in the text, and they had to assume the meaning of uncertain words.

Reading the text the pupils met various difficulties, such as the loss of attention, unknown words, and the psychological problems, like shyness to asks questions or read aloud. For example, one boy was felt shy reading aloud. But being a shy pupil at reading out aloud he did not show any weaknesses in oral English. Having analysed the post-reading exercise, the author concluded that the poor comprehenders were slower and less accurate at making logical conclusions and casual relationships. The thing which united the poor comprehenders was the difficulty to find the semantic meaning. Another general problem was the pupils' inability to make inferences. The failure to draw conclusions was likely to seriously complicate comprehension. For example, the post-reading exercise results showed that some readers still confused wild animals with domestic ones.

The post-reading test demonstrated that the weak readers had difficulties in drawing conclusions. On the other hand, the poor readers failed to make conclusions not because they were unable to do so, but simply because of the failure to remember the facts appeared in the text earlier.

Doing the post-reading exercise, some students were unable to understand the instructions in English. The problem was related to special terms like "word", "adjective", "sentence". These words tend to be used in my instructions. But many children had difficulty in understanding them, because these terms were not easily related to the spoken language. In such cases, instructions were given in their native language.

Table 3.3 **The third experimental lesson's plan**

Sequence	Time (minutes)	Activity	Content
1	5	Warm-up activities	Homework analysis, warm-up questions
2	10	Pre-reading	A semantic map
3	5	Reading a letter	A students' letter home
4	5	while-reading	Comprehension questions
5	10	Post-reading	Roleplay
6	5	Homework explanation	-

The objectives of the lesson were: to acquire grammar patterns and vocabulary items, to read and understand the text, to apply the group task, to speak about school subjects.

The tasks of the lesson were: to read the text and find the information, to ask and answer the questions about the text, to study new words, to act a conversation.

Before reading the text the author explained new words written on the board: college, video rental shop, settle down, share, lonely. The students practiced the pronunciation of them.

Secondly, the author paper introduced the topic of the reading lesson. The author started the lesson with general warm-up questions, such as" Who is absent today? ","Are you ready for another reading lesson? "," What are your favourite heroes?", ,, Where did you meet them?" The author inquired them about stories, tales they had ever read.

The pre-reading exercise consisted of the discussion on the titles presented on the semantic map. The semantic map was written on the blackboard and contained the names of school subjects taught at all school levels. The pupils were discussing them. Having discussed school subjects, the students started reading one student's letter home. The author asked them some while-reading comprehension questions, such as "Where does a student study?", "How many lessons does she have every day?"

Having read the text they started doing the post-reading exercise. As a post-reading exercise the students were asked to do a roleplay. The author introduced the context of the roleplay: Beverly, a cousin of Natalie's, is in London and telephones Natalie to find out how she is setting down, she asks about the Wilson family, their house, Dover and Natalie's plans. The students were asked to elicit a selection of questions which Beverly might ask. The author wrote these on the board, divided the class into pairs and told those who had the part of Natalie to prepare what they are going to say in answer to each question. The author told those who had the part of Beverly to practice the questions. Students did the role-play in pairs and wrote the conversation out for homework.

It was not possible to get a true assessment of a child's ability by measuring what she or he could do alone without help and interaction with others. The correct answers were assessed by giving them marks. The criteria were: How natural was the students' speed in reading? How well did the students complete the task? How many common mistakes (grammar, lexis, pronunciation) did the student make? Were there serious mistakes for this level?

The analysis of the lesson. The most common difficulty was to follow the plan prepared. Poor vocabulary, mean abilities to draw conclusions, inattention were the main reasons for the plan gap. This lesson was no exception.

The semantic map presented before reading, focused the pupils' attention on what they were about to read and clarified their thoughts about the topic of the letter. The semantic map was evidently a good motivational material which gained their interest in reading.

The author used skimming and scanning in while-reading exercises. Skimming was used so that the students could get the general contents of the text. After having skimmed the text, the students could study the text in more details, reading more slowly, carefully and looking for information in order to answer specific questions about the text. They had to use scanning. The purpose of comprehension questions was to check that the students did the reading assignment and they understood it. The author used pre-questions that served to focus the students' attention on the important points of the letter during the reading. The questions prepared by the author had many positive features. They were answerable with information quoted directly from the reading selection. (WH – questions – who, when, where, what).

2. They were answerable with information acquired from the reading selection, usually why or how- questions. The author gave the class opportunity to talk in a controlled situation where the answers were simply lifted from the reading. However, there were some not so good points. The students had to speak the answers rather than just read them and it could be considered as an exercise in improving short memory rather than in reading.

While reading the letter, the readers got most of the letter text from skimming the topic sentences. But skimming was not easy for the children, who read slowly. The author has also discovered, that reading comprehension was strongly related to their knowledge about the particular features of the letter, such as the beginning, the ending, and the title. Most of the skilled readers gave the examples of the particular information contained in the letter, such as "the main subjects were", "the work days are". But only about a half of the poor readers of the class could perform so. The main reason for this is that the poor readers considered that titles, beginnings and endings provided little useful information. They also did not believe that the beginnings of the narratives might present worthy information about its characters, causes. The author also asked the class to repeat the sentences read. It was evident that the weak readers repeated fewer sentences correctly. Even though the task required only word-for-word repetition, verbal memory weakness was plain.

In the end, the author asked the class to do a roleplay. One of the aspects of reading as an active skill is its communicative function. On the elementary level students have a limited vocabulary and in the conversation they used ready made structures which helped them to increase their vocabulary. This exercise was meaningful, however, it was evident that the weak readers made fewer sentences correctly.

To assess the students the author has used student - centered approach, their participation in all activities, social aspect of learning.

The total analysis of the three experimental lessons.

During the pedagogical practice the author got acquainted with the students, observed teaching strategies and students' learning attitudes. The author got to know the range of students' abilities, discussed the school's resources, materials, teaching resources, programmes and policies, studied the theoretical materials. The author evaluated his lessons, discussed the ways to improve the teaching techniques, diagnosed the knowledge and skills of the students and modified programmes accordingly. During the practice the author continued to consolidate his teaching skills previously developed.

Finally, the marks received at the three experimental lessons have been studied. Figure 3.3 shows these results, where the vertical axis reflects the coefficients of the students' comprehension in reading.

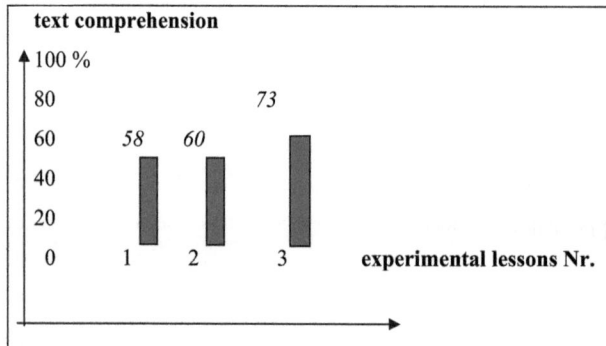

Figure.3.3. **The evaluation of the text comprehension.**

The students showed the middle and the high levels of the text comprehension during the three experimental lessons. However, it is necessary to note, that the last lesson's text comprehension was averagely at a high level.

CHAPTER 4

Having analysed the experimental lessons, the research paper author made the following conclusions. Motivation is one of the leading factors improving the reading skills. The better motivated students usually have more chances to become skilled readers. Practically, a more interesting text was going to be more motivating to read, but difficult words in the text, too complicated grammar reduced pupils` interest in reading. The experimental lessons proved the idea that when the concerned background was familiar, poor readers drew less logical conclusions form the text. They sometimes had different goals when reading the text, focusing on reading individual words rather than understanding the meaning. The author has also discovered, that reading comprehension was strongly related to their knowledge about the particular features of a text, such as the beginning, the ending, and the title. It is necessary to note, that the poor readers considered that titles, beginnings and endings provided little useful information. Some of them so far forgot to take advantage of post-reading instructions like "if you are not sure of an answer, go on to the next question", "answer the easier questions first and then go back to the harder question". Instead of this they focused their attention on a single question encountered.

Having analysed the theoretical ideas, the research paper author made the following conclusions. Some researches consider that memorizing whole words may lead to rapid progress in early reading, particularly for children with good visual memories. Others state that the children, who were taught phonics, exhibited the early advantage of word recognition, particularly in untaught words. Both the methods must be used in order to achieve high results in improving reading skills.

When readers become more experienced and confident, they use skimming and scanning approaches effectively. Skimming and scanning are two approaches to reading which can be useful for specific purposes (getting a general idea, or finding specific information).

Before performing a particular exercise student's prior knowledge should be activated. There are various kinds of pre-reading activities, such as focus questions, content analysis, graphic organizers, and semantic maps, thought webs, pyramid outlines and anticipation guides. The choice of the pre-reading activities depends on the purpose of reading. The while-reading stage is to help learners to understand the text. By answering teacher's questions students determine what they do not understand and what they need to clarify. Some tables, semantic maps may be written on the blackboard while pupils are reading. By all means teachers should help learners to understand the text rather than just test their comprehension constantly. The final part of the effective reading is post-reading strategies. As usual, the oral part of the post-reading strategies consists of "who", "what", "when", "where" questions about the material pupils have just read. Some experts believe that good post-reading activities usually involve listening or speaking and sometimes writing. The choice of the post-reading activities depends on the purpose of reading.

The major psychological problems of the struggling readers are diffidence, shyness, and complexes. The author of the paper was not surprised when he found out that most of his less successful students had these psychological difficulties. The last inference is that poor-conclusion making ability and poor vocabulary is main the cause of poor reading and language comprehension.

In the process of the research the author of the paper had come across some difficulties, such as lack of methodological literature on teaching reading at basic school. The author of the research paper recommends using the tasks and activities which are tailored according to the students 'cognitive interests and needs, level of English knowledge and their cultural backgrounds.

The research that was carried out based on the author's analysis of the theoretical literature and his practical experience, allow the author to ascertain that the hypothesis of the paper has been proved. The application of the effective reading methods that correspond to the needs and the interests of the students improves their reading comprehension and increase their interest in reading.

LIST OF LITERATURE

1. Christopher Brumfit, Ronald Carter. Literature and Language Teaching. - London: Oxford University Press, 1987. -191,192 p.

2. Coreen Sears. Second Language Students in Mainstream Classrooms: A Handbook for Teachers in International Schools. - Clevedon, England: Multilingual Matters Ltd, 1998. - 165 p.

3. David A. Sousa. How the Brain Learns to Read. - Thousand Oaks, USA: Corwin Press, 2004. 6-142 p.

4. Deborah P. Berrill, Dirk Jan Verhulst, Laura Doucette. Tutoring Adolescent Readers. - Markham, Canada: Pembroke Publishers, 2006. 68-93 p.

5. Democratic approach to school development: involving all interest groups // Journal of teachers education and training: Volume 6 / Lukk.K, Veisson. M, Ruus. V, Sarv. E. - Tallin University, 1996. - 96 p.

6. Dennis M. McInerney. Developmental psychology for teachers: An Applied Approach. - Sydney: Allen & Unwin, 2006. - 137 p.

7. Donald Bear. Developing Literacy: An Integrated Approach to Assessment and Instruction. - Boston: Houghton Mifflin Company, 1998. - 208 p.

8. Embracing Diversity in the Learning Sciences: Proceedings of the Sixth International Conference of the Learning Sciences / Yasmin.B.Kafai, William.A.Sandoval, Noel Enyedy, Althea Scott Nixon, Francisco Herrera. - New Jersey: Lawrence Erlbaum, 2004. - 443 p.

9. Goldman L. Raising Our Children to be Resilient: A Guide to Helping Children Cope with Trauma in Today's world. - New York: Brunner-Routledge, 2005. - 35 p.

10. Herbert Ira London. Decade of denial : A Snapshot of America in the 1990s.- Lanham, USA: Lexington Books, 2001. - 45 p.

11. James Hoffman, Dianne L Shallert. The texts in elementary classrooms. - Mahwah: Lawrence Erlbaum Associates, 2004. - 61, 62 p.

12. Jane Braunger, Jan Patricia Lewis. Building a knowledge base in reading. - 1 st. edition. - Newark, DE: International Reading Association, 1997. - 72 p.

13. Jessie Wise, Sara Buffington. The Ordinary Parent's Guide to Teaching Reading.-Charles City, USA: Peace Hill Press, 2004. 356-358 p.

14. Jo Phenix. The Reading Teacher's Handbook. - Markham, Canada: Pembroke Publishers, 2002. - 16 p.

15. Judith Orasanu.Reading Comprehension: From Research to Practice. - Hillsdale, USA: Lawrence Erlbaum Associates, 1986. -1 p.

16. Kalat J.W. Introduction to Psychology. - 4th ed. Pacific Grove. - CA: Brooks/Cole Publ. Co, 1996. - 375 p.

17. Keith Rayner, Alexander Pollatsek. The Psychology of Reading. - Prentice-Hall, USA: Lawrence Erlbaum, 1994. 23-348 p.

18. Lisa Oakley. Cognitive development. - London: Routledge, 2004. -29 p.

19. Lori Jamison Rog. Guided Reading Basics: Organizing, Managing, and Implementing a Balanced Literacy Program in K-3.- Markham, USA: Stenhouse Publishers, 2003. 144-149 p.

20. Marilyn Jager Adams. Beginning to Read: Thinking and Learning about Print. - Cambridge: The MIT Press, 1994.- 38 p.

21. Michael Pressley. Reading Instruction That Works. - New York: Guilford Press, 1998. 154-418 p.

22. Michael W. Eysenck. Psychology: An International Perspective. - New York: Psychology Press, 2004. - 531 p.

23. Paul Davies, Eric Pearse. Success in English Teaching. - London: Oxford University Press, 2000. 93-100 p.

24. Pipere. A. Education & sustainable development. - Daugavpils: "Saule", 2006.-70 p.

25. Rik Ruiter, Pinky Dang. Highway To E.S.L.: A User-Friendly Guide to Teaching English As A Second Language. - New York, Universe, Inc, 2005. - 125 p.

26. Robert D. Postman. Barron's How to Prepare for the Praxis. -3 rd edition. -New York: Barrons Educational Series Inc, 2005. - 332 p.

27. Roger.D.Sell. Children's Literature as Communication: The Chilpa Project.-Philadelphia, USA: John Benjamins Publishing Co, 2002. - 304 p.

28. Rona F. Filipo. Reading Researchers in Search of Common Ground, - Newark, DE: International Reading Association, 2001. -137 p.

29. Rosalie Fink. Why Jane and John Couldn't Read-And How They Learned: A New Look at Striving Readers. -Newark, DE: International Reading Association, 2006. - 26 p.

30. Schaffer H Rudolph, Rodgers B Bryan, Adamowicz Wik. Introducing Child Psychology. - London: Blackwell Publishers, 2003. - 177 p.

31. Susan B. Neuman, David K. Dickinson Handbook of Early Literacy Research, - Volume 1. - New York: The Guilford Press, 2003. - 59 p.

32. Thomas P. Rohlen, Christopher Björk. Education and training in Japan.-London: Routledge, 1998. - 174 p.
33. Timothy V. Rasinski, Nancy D. Motivating Recreational Reading and Promoting Home-School Connections. -Newark, DE: International Reading Association, 2000.- 1 p.
34. Vincent Douglas, Marjorie M. Smith. Total Basic Skills, Grade 6. -Wilson Drive, USA: American Education Publishing, 2004. - 51 p.
35. Psiholoģijas un pedagoģijas pamati: populārs pamatkurss / Koemetss. E, Tamma. L, Elango. A, Indre.K - Rīga : Zvaigzne, 1984. - 99 p.
36. А. Воробьёв. Психология.-Рига: Zvaigzne ABC, 1996.- 63 p.
37. English alphabet. -http://en.wikipedia.org/wiki/English_alphabet
38. Phonics methods.- http://www.teachingtreasures.com.au/homeschool/reading-methods/reading-methods.htm#phonics
39. Pronunciation of the sounds. - http://www.omniglot.com/writing/english.htm
40. The searching engine.- www.google.com/books

Appendix 1

Letter names (37)

Letter	Letter name (pronunciation)
A	a /eɪ/
B	bee /bi:/
C	cee /si:/
D	dee /di:/
E	e /i:/
F	ef /ɛf/ (spelled *eff* as a verb)
G	gee /dʒi:/
H	aitch /eɪtʃ/; or /heɪtʃ/ (*haitch*) in Hiberno-English and sometimes Australian and British English
I	i /aɪ/
J	jay /dʒeɪ/; sometimes *jy* /dʒaɪ/ in Scottish English and elsewhere.
K	kay /keɪ/
L	el /ɛl/
M	em /ɛm/
N	en /ɛn/
O	o /oʊ/
P	pee /pi:/
Q	cue /kju:/
R	ar /ɑr/ (*see rhotic and non-rhotic accents*)
S	ess /ɛs/ (spelled *es-* in compounds like *es-hook*)
T	tee /ti:/
U	u /ju:/
V	vee /vi:/
W	double-u /)(`dʌb(ə)l ju:/
X	ex /ɛks/
Y	wye /waɪ/
Z	zed /zɛd/; zee /zi:/ in American English; formerly also *izzard*

Appendix 2

A handy alphabet table(37)

a - ape a - antelope a - armadillo b - bear c - civet c - cat d - deer e - emu e - elephant f - fox g - gerbil g - goldfish	h - hippopotamus i - ibis i - inchworm j - jaguar k - kangaroo l - lizard m - monkey n - nightingale o - okapi o - ostrich p - peacock q - quail	r - rabbit s - snake t - tiger u - unicorn u - umbrella bird v - vole w - walrus x - ox y - butterfly y - yak z - zebra

Appendix. 3

Pronunciation (39)

Vowels

ɑː   father ['fɑːðə], alms [ɑːmz], clerk [klɑːk], heart [hɑːt], sergeant ['sɑːdʒənt]
æ   cat [kæt], plait [plæt]
ɛ   bet [bɛt], ate [ɛt], bury ['bɛrɪ], heifer ['hɛfə], said [sɛd], says [sɛz]
ə   potter ['pɒtə], alone [ə'ləʊn], furious ['fjʊərɪəs], nation ['neɪʃən], the [ðə]
ɜː   fern [fɜːn], burn [bɜːn], fir [fɜː], learn [lɜːn], term [tɜːm], worm [wɜːm]
ɪ   pretty ['prɪtɪ], build [bɪld], busy ['bɪzɪ], nymph [nɪmf], pocket ['pɒkɪt], sieve [sɪv], women ['wɪmɪn]
iː   see [siː], aesthete ['iːsθiːt], evil ['iːvəl], magazine [ˌmægə'ziːn], receive [rɪ'siːv] siege [siːdʒ]
ɒ   pot [pɒt], botch [bɒtʃ], sorry ['sɒrɪ]
ɔː   thaw [θɔː], broad [brɔːd], drawer ['drɔːə], fault [fɔːlt], halt [hɔːlt], organ ['ɔːgən]
ʊ   pull [pʊl], good [gʊd], should [ʃʊd], woman ['wʊmən]
uː   zoo [zuː], do [duː], queue [kjuː], shoe [ʃuː], spew [spjuː], true [truː], you [juː]
ʌ   cut [kʌt], flood [flʌd], rough [rʌf], son [sʌn]

Diphthongs and triphthongs

aɪ   dive [daɪv], aisle [aɪl], guy [gaɪ], might [maɪt], rye [raɪ]
aɪə   fire ['faɪə], buyer ['baɪə], liar ['laɪə], tyre ['taɪə]
aʊ   out [aʊt], bough [baʊ], crowd [kraʊd], slouch [slaʊtʃ]
aʊə   flour ['flaʊə], cower ['caʊə], flower ['flaʊə], sour ['saʊə]
eɪ   paid [peɪd], day [deɪ], deign [deɪn], gauge [geɪdʒ], grey [greɪ], neigh [neɪ]
ɛə   bear [bɛə], dare [dɛə], prayer [prɛə], stairs [stɛəz], where [wɛə]
ɪə   tear [tɪə], beer [bɪə], mere [mɪə], tier [tɪə]
oʊ   note [noʊt], beau [boʊ], dough [doʊ], hoe [hoʊ], slow [sloʊ] yeoman ['jəʊmən]
ɔɪ   void [vɔɪd], boy [bɔɪ], destroy [dɪ'strɔɪ]
ʊə   poor [pʊə], skewer ['skjʊə], sure [ʃʊə]

Appendix.4

Pronunication (39)

Consonants

- p   **p**ig [pɪg]   b **b**ig [bɪg]   t **t**ea [tiː]   d **d**actylology [ˌdæktɪ'lɒlədʒɪ]
- k   **k**angaroo [ˌkæŋgə'ɹuː], **c**acophony [kə'kɒfənɪ]
- g   **g**et [gɛt], **gh**oul [guːl], **gu**ard [gaːd], e**x**amine [ɪ'gzæmɪn]
- m   **m**amm**o**th ['mæməθ]
- n   **n**yctophobia [ˌnɪktəʊ'fəʊbɪə], **kn**owledge ['nɒlɪdʒ], **gn**otobiotics [ˌnəʊtəʊbaɪ'ɒtɪks], **pn**eumatic ['njʊmætɪk]
- ŋ   si**ng** [sɪŋ], phary**n**x ['fæɹɪŋks]
- ɹ   **r**adio ['ɹeɪdɪəʊ], **rh**inoceros [ɹaɪ'nɒsəɹəs / ɹaɪ'nɒsɹəs]
- f   **f**oxtrot ['fɒksˌtrɒt], **ph**oenix ['fiːnɪks]   v **v**arious ['vɛəɹɪəs]
- θ   **th**in [θɪn]   ð **th**ese [ðiːz]
- s   **s**illy ['sɪlɪ], **c**ircus ['sɜːkəs]   z **z**ebra ['ziːbɹə / 'zɛbrə], **X**erox ['zɪəɹɒks]
- ʃ   **sh**ip [ʃɪp], elec**ti**on [ɪ'lɛkʃən], ma**ch**ine [mə'ʃiːn], mi**ss**ion ['mɪʃən], pre**ss**ure ['pɹɛʃə], **sch**edule ['ʃɛdjuːl]
- ʒ   trea**s**ure ['tɹɛʒə], a**z**ure ['æʒə], eva**s**ion [ɪ'veɪʒən]
- h   **h**otel [həʊ'tɛl]
- l   **l**atera**l** ['lætəɹəl]
- j   **y**es [jɛs], on**i**on ['ʌnjən], v**i**gnette [vɪ'njɛt]
- tʃ   **ch**ew [tʃuː], na**t**ure ['neɪtʃə]
- dʒ   **j**aw [dʒɔː], a**dj**ective ['ædʒɪktɪv], sol**di**er ['səʊldʒə], usa**ge** ['juːsɪdʒ]
- w   **w**et [wɛt], **wh**eel [wiːl]

Appendix.5

Phonics method (38)

1) a-t   i-t   o-n   i-f   b-e   m-e   n-o   w-e   i-n   h-e

c-a-t   s-a-t   m-a-t   f-a-t   p-a-t   r-a-t   c-a-r   g-o-d

m-e-n

f-l-a-t   p-l-a-t   t-h-a-t   s-p-i-t   g-r-i-t   s-l-i-t

2) The cat sat on the mat.   3) The hen is in a pen

Appendix.6

Pupils interview

Teacher: "Why don't you like reading in the classroom?"

V:" I don't like reading to the class as much as I like reading to myself".

K: "I get all mix up when I read it out aloud".

J: "I like reading but I always expect grammar exercises after it".

D: "I understand the meaning of the words, but I'm afraid of my pronunciation".

Teacher: "Do you read English books at home?"

R: "No, I don't read in English, because I've to go in for sports".

N: "I read only the texts connected with my homework".

A: "My mother really helps me in reading, because her English is better than mine".

K: "I like watching cartoons in English rather than reading, it's a little bit boring".

I: "I understand that I must read in English, but I expend much time in my homework. I don't spend much time in reading."

Teacher:" What do you like to read about?"

D: "I'd like to know about the stars and planets."

K: "I'm interested in cooking."

R: "I can't reply to you at once, maybe computer techniques".

I: "I prefer short tales."